The Bramble King

The Bramble King

Catherine Fisher

Seren is the book imprint of
Poetry Wales Press Ltd.
57 Nolton Street, Bridgend, Wales, CF31 3AE
www.serenbooks.com
facebook.com/SerenBooks
twitter@SerenBooks

The right of Catherine Fisher to be identified as
the author of this work has been asserted in accordance
with the Copyright, Designs and Patents Act, 1988.

ISBN: 978-1-78172-507-8
ebook: 978-1-78172-508-5
Kindle: 978-1-78172-509-2

A CIP record for this title is available from the British Library.

The publisher acknowledges the financial assistance of the Welsh Books Council.

Cover painting: Detail from 'Primavera' by Sandro Botticelli,
Photograph by Peter Schmidbauer.

Author Photograph: © Rachel Davies Photography.

Printed in Bembo by Latimer Trend & Company Ltd, Plymouth.

Contents

Imaginary Planets

1. Hades

Where the sky flames all day, all night,
and carbon horses draw the cars of death.
Where the nightmares of men might come
after they are dreamed.

A destination so remote a traveller
would arrive as his own grandson.

Out in a lost arm of the galaxy,
never seen in Hubble.
Plotted by some disbelieving researcher
late at night in a deserted room,
stopping to take his glasses off and rub his eyes
and stare at the lists of figures
as if for a moment he had thought he'd seen...
but no
       Surely not.

2. Temenos

I think I've been there.
One of those slants of dread that come at three am
when the room shivers you awake.

No one but lost ships and losers.
Automated freight gone missing from the screens.
The sky is grey, the soil grey,
dying trees are wreathed in mist.

There might have to be a world like this
to holiday the incurably optimistic,
the climate-change sceptic,
the spoiled, the oiled, the never been hungry.
Everyone else just changes ships and goes.

The odd thing is, it's not silent.
There are cries at night, as if from tall birds
stalking out there in the shadowy marshes,
gaunt shapes with silent silvery wings
asking questions, calling someone's name.

3. Babel

No one lands there; if they did they would go mad.
There are species there that talk, animals
and birds, each with a voice, a view, a conversation.
There are voices everywhere, singing and crying,
giving opinions, and no one listens,
listening is not what it's about at all.
They say, once, a girl was shipwrecked,
surviving in the spaceship's broken hull
all alone, for a year. She had food, water,
in a strange way, company.
        When they got to her at last she had no words,
no meanings, no syllables, no poetry.
She squalked and whistled, howled and trumpeted.
No one understood what she was saying.
The doctors asked her questions.
Peered in her mouth and ears, took notes, took scans.
"Nothing" they said, "nothing is wrong with her."

She looked at them as if their songs were broken.

4. Gravitas

It's too heavy. You weigh a hundred pounds.
Each arm takes centuries to raise, each breath

a year to breathe. The effort to lift your eyelids
ages you by stealth.

Don't sit down, you can't get up.
Don't sleep, you'll never wake.

And your words, they come out low and slow
in the deepest bass, as if the world

would pull them down, and you,
like magnets to the molten iron core.

5. Circe

He came in past the Sirens
and maybe they sang but it was safe
because there is no sound in space.

In the polarized perspex of his helmet
their lips reflected like opened crators;
through the crashing orbits

of Scylla and Charybdis
the ship fell and far below
a world all blue, all ocean,

and in its heart a jewel,
the only landing station. She has been waiting
centuries. It was all he could ask for,

though the wave-washed dome was cold
and the rooms echoed with the ghosts
of transformed men.

She fed him figs and berries,
unlaced his silver suit.
She could keep him here forever, she said,

and he'd stay young and laugh at memories.
But late at night on the blue shore he sat
staring at the stars, his legend calling him.

He pleaded. She warned him
he'd been gone too long,
light-years had been woven and unpicked.

So when he blasted off in his patched capsule
she knew he'd be back, tumbling from terror,
unable to escape her gravity.

6. Planet X

It must be there. Something occludes
the star's light. Something huge

and dark, passing between us,
spacetime distorted by its mass.

Behind the eyepiece of my telescope,
– you on the hemisphere of sleep –

we chart its bent spectra.
What climate, what species, I wonder

inhabit that darkness
only instruments show?

I want to ask you, but the subtle
horizon drags your signal

so far around it's blurred.
How can a world be unheard,

how could it orbit out there all our lives?
I'm afraid of what we've discovered.

Call me. Tell me
you see it too.

The Shop

1. Corridor of Glass

There are slants and angles of faces and they move
as she moves. The stacked panes in the corridor
are faceted, razor-edged, alert.

Filth and web don't blunt the jagged corners.
A slip means sliced fingers. It's forbidden
even to be here, in these dim reflected dangers.

But there's the door, secret and forgotten,
opening behind the shelves of tins of paint,
Crown and Dulux, Magnolia and Mimosa,

where her eye to the slit shows customers
or the old men who sit
in her grandfather's chair, their voices thin as bleats.

They don't know she's here. A small creak
would betray her. Invisible, a glass girl,
she sees the world in slivers, the enigmatic adults,

the people passing in the rainy street. Eye to a slit,
not sure of anything, catching words and fragments
endlessly mirrored. She'll grow up. Nothing will change.

2. Under the Stairs

Under the stairs was a cubbyhole choked with paper.
Wallpaper rolls, scrunched borders, a head-high hiding place
she had to crawl or wriggle through, make tunnels in,

the stickiness of paste, offcuts of people's rooms,
curled rejected choices, colours splashed to try.
A clotted mass, she breathed it, a forest of fibres

to drifts that sank, got trampled, then more thrown in and more,
whose new leaves cascaded down each year
until, one work-less winter, they cleared it

to a small white space. So small! A bench along it.
And her grandfather, leaning on the brush saying "That's where
we sat the bombs out." Ceilinged with stairs,

she thought "Who could that save?" Its whiteness pleased.
But after only days the paper started back. She knew
it would fill up again like the days fill, like a lifetime, piling,

shred by shred, colour by colour, scrap by scrap,
like the drafts of a novel that'll never get written,
the small bench bombed and buried below memory.

3. Sweeping

When the bell sounded after the last customer
she found the brush and swept behind the counter.

Slices of wallpaper, curliques and scraps
deep as the leaves in an autumn heap.

Some of it sticky with paste, some torn,
textures of artex and polystyrene

velvety swirls of flock, the William Morris
birds, the crunched brown forests.

Somewhere in there the banknotes,
the pounds and ten shillings she had to sort

like treasure in the tales, like finds in a dig.
Sweeping up the day's detritus

the lifetime's offcuts, as if the shop
hoarded all the things left, the unwanted corners,

the unloved ends. They would make a pile
as big as the world, they would rustle

all round her and be hard and rough
and the bin was never never big enough.

Solstice

This is the needle-eye of winter,
the sun tugged though it like a knot.

Thin end of the wedge, acute angle,
the place where ceiling meets floor.

Here you have to crawl. Here the year
is hammered flat, reminted.

This is the day of long straight shadows
out from the heels of houses,

the day that blinds drivers, marble of light
rolling the horizon

between chapel and shop.
Druids at Stonehenge sings as it drops,

token in a Neolithic game.
In the tomb at Newgrange

sixteen lucky people drawn by lot
crouch in an ache of awe

watching winter go down the wall.
The moment is too small.

Owl Pellet Poem

Perched in the dark, she chokes this out,
coughs this up. It's packed tight:
fluff, fur, crammed bones, skulls.
Tiny teeth. Eggshells.

You'll find, if you prise it apart,
all the stuff that hurts;
her gristle and splinters,
inedible beaks and claws.

What she snatches away, what she preys on,
What she's eaten.
What she's cursed and kissed.
What she's destroyed for this.

It's out. Now she can chance
the scorned and longed-for silence.

The Daughter of the Sun

The daughter of the Sun is in her tower.
The doors are locked. Not one beam of light
can pierce the walls. She's stacking up the furniture,
chairs on tables; look, the cat's basket,
the sofa upended, wobbly stools, benches.
She's making a steep staircase of the stuff
piled on her life, and she's kicked off her shoes,
is climbing fast, faster than it's safe,

on squashy cushions, hauled up by her fingers,
scrambling up the whole collapsing heap.
Surely there's a thin unshuttered window.
Is it imagination? Is the air rarer up
here, is there a draught? Now she can see her hands,
there's a glint of gold, his fire,
slanting the darkness like a sword,
gilding her face and fingers.

 The daughter of the Sun has found the window.
She pulls the latch, the casement clatters open.
From her wobbly silence she sees slow
barges on a serpent river, a forest of pine
and mountains rising, grey and gold. There
is his kingdom, and she laughs because she'll take it,
she'll inherit, though they batter down the door,

though she has to fly, though the ground is far,
her wings as frail as clouds, wide as winter.

Sion's Seat

Go early while the dew's still on it.
Take the river path, up the rushing way
past dippers and wagtail.
Heron's eye, yellow as celandine
sees you sidelong, whole head attent.

Into the wood by mossy stones, the track
mud, the pools of splash.
Under trees that knot and crouch,
that make the valley a green crevice,
a lichened slot in the land.

Ignore the bridge. Go up
on the switchback path, the track
zedding on itself, zigzagging high,
till the rocks outcrop and breath comes short
and where the heart hurts, Sion's seat.

Who were you, Sion, dead at twenty,
your couch a green cromlech,
velvet with moss, oozing water,
dripping with small grey
shrews that dive in the cracks?

Grave without stanza, *bedd heb englyn*,
tilted bed of a wood-walker.
Never knew you, Sion, but the trees
stand by you, and the kickback
path is the run-off of your spent silence.

I think you might have been a big guy,
Bran-like. I sit in your lap.
Your green knees spread; roots
your bones that break through the soil,
small insects swarm in your veins.

Easy to think of you mythic, mighty,
the crumpled valleys your body,
some silent Arthur still up here.
But the plaque is tilted and may not last long.
The lichen eating your name, Sion.

Two Poems for February

1. Cold

I know it has fingers. Can see
the designs they scrape on the window.
There are other things I know;
how it strikes deep, stiffens the body

to a puppet, jerky, controlled.
Bells in empty towers hang with ice,
a bird skitters on silence.
Even the young look old.

Through my grey wood, over the fields,
no leaf falls, no starling rises.
It's not anarchy, more like some lost project,
a plan that died at the outset,
a fallen coin on the pavement
no one will unglove to collect.

2. Frost

Minutes ago it lay on the tarmac,
a glinting powder.
Now only slant shadows of bollards preserve it.
Negative of normality.
Zigzag of cold and thaw.

Last night, around the uncoloured moon
a corona prophesied its coming;
made of rainbow, withheld breath
of the stark sky.

This is an art deco winter,
all monochrome, all angles,
the streets cornered,
their edges neatly aligned
as if nuance no longer counts,
as if some deep geometric truth
has come out in the cold.

It reminds me of the small black clock
I dreamed of in the night,
marquesite hands admonishing,
with sharp terse ticks,
the white face of the world.

Post-War

I love that image of Wynford Vaughan-Thomas
finding the stored paintings in Montegufoni;
proud refugees saying "Giotto, si, e Uccello"
and his shout of joy, his "*My God, Botticelli!*"
And there she is, upside-down maybe,
dusty and almost forgotten, but there she is,
Flora with flowers spilling from her mouth,
Spring with hand raised and the red dress,
the dancing muses, the garden of fruit.
There she is, out of the old illustrations,
come round again, Europe's darling.
And everyone standing there grinning.
Despite the dead. Despite everything.

Adam

In the life class someone's brought a book.
Before the model comes we gather round it.
The pages turn. No one speaks.
There's a silence that says everything.

We put him in the pose and he tries hard
but his physique's not great. It's just as well,
because our lines are hesitant and scared,
defining what we think we ought to see

and never can. In sanguine chalks and inks,
in pen and wash, with smudgy charcoal fingers
we reach out eternally and make
languid imperfect men in our own image.

During the tea break I sneak back to look.
Nothing is alive. No one's moved.

Dancers

Today he draws Eve. She dips her toe in powder
knowing he's watching. Points it, arches,
dirty satin gleaming. His fingers
move, rainbowed with dust.

Yesterday I was on that paper;
soft crumbly strokes on grey, my arms
silent marks. "Forget I'm here" he says;
I can't, his gaze dissolves me

to lines and blurs, fixes my brief turns,
stills an art gone in seconds,
all leap and heartbeat. On tiny
smudgy pages squeezes and contracts us,

rubbing our edges smooth.
"Move" he says, "Don't stop." Wants
angles, drifting talk, a draught.
Forgets we're here. Draws us from the mirrors.

Edgar Degas Caught on a Loop of Film

In the last room of the exhibition, a screen.
After all the arabesques and chiffon
here the picture moves, and you are still.

He walks toward you down the boulevard.
A woman smiles, a man turns to look.
You're the camera. Your shadow angles the pavement.

He's blind now. A gentleman with hat and cane
walking with the careful emphasis of age.
But he still knows the triumphs of the body,

the languorous neck, the muscles of the arm;
drew them as if they'd never be enough;
trapeze artists and dancers and jockeys

straining for perfection, for release
for whatever it is that lies beyond the moment,
for whatever will be left.

Just when he gets to you, he looks up, flickers,
jumps back to the start. You watch him walk again,
uneasy, feeling the cruelty of it.

The House to its Owner

Sell me the house says, sell me.
I'm tired of you.
The way you neglect me,
don't quite see me any more.
The way you gaze through me every night
as if you wanted something else.

You've been a disappointment, the house says,
spent nothing on me.
I creak, my roof drizzles.
All my doors are warped.
I can't get warm. My original features
are only visible in mirrors.

Listen, I snap, listen. You were finished, a ruin,
give me credit for patching you up.
You don't help, always getting mildew,
your garden brambled,
your outhouses collapsing in every storm.

I want someone new, the house says,
who'll see potential, not dismay.
With kids, with a dog,
someone younger with a bit of vision.

I would answer, but in the unfinished double glazing
my two mouths are kissing out of synch.

The Tenant's Mail

It clogs the door. Slides on the floor.
His phone bills. Letters from banks.
Pizza leaflets. *As one of our valued customers...*

Gathered, it has a faint dust.
Envelopes grit on each other.
Damp stamps curl like disdain.

I carry them into the kitchen
and see where he's left the cleaning things;
a new mop. Unused kettle.

His brochures are exotic. Thailand.
China, where he told me he was going,
giving up work, selling everything.

You have won... Are you in debt?
Is your life going nowhere?
How do I forward this? Not to mention

the six letters in red biro
all on the same creamy stationery,
with his name looped in a childish scrawl.

He's left the keys on a string by the door.
They swing. As if he'd only just gone past them.
As if his draught had moved them.

The Flat Where the Cinema Was

You'd think it would be the noises she would hear;
explosions, car chases,
crackle of gunfire sprayed across her sleep.
Or the roaring orchestrated minute
when the rowing couple get to kiss.
You'd think it would be this.

But it's the quiet. Pointed pauses
in the conversation. That angry face-off.
Second just before the pistol fires.
And through the windows, like applause,
always the slo-mo pigeons.

She finds she doesn't need the television;
only has to dim the lights. And there's the hero
gazing at the girl across her room.
She cooks and eats, her shadow huge on close-up lips.
Wise-cracking. Chewed cigars. Threats.

In bed she sleeps among the other couples,
a rapid flicker of embraces.
Horsemen ride across her hall.
And words, jerky words
on rectangles of darkness, never still,
placard her afternoons with exclamations.

The Houses Where the School Was

There was a particular piece of corridor,
a turning just before the toilets, by a cupboard in the wall,
I knew was haunted. On those rainy afternoons
when the building was stale with smell of cooking,
sleepy kids would pause there.
No one said why. There were no stories.

Now it's hard to find that place; it lies between
someone's front gate and their plastic door,
or maybe where the wheelie bin is propped.
Rain falls here now; the floorboard creak is gone,
the direction you had to come from altered.

That place has moved; migrated to memory
in maybe a thousand people, lessening yearly.
Now I'm the ghost that haunts it, standing here
trying to work out where it used to be.
Maybe the kids and I on the long queue from the yard
sensed this fence, this scruffy garden. Maybe we knew
someone would come and reconfigure all our lives.

Tidal

Let's join and ebb then like the tide.
Touch and leave.
Let's whisper like the slow withdrawing wave.

Down there the fluid mud
firms and murmurs and delays,
stirs small coiled eddies in its heart.
Down there the dissolved salt
is held, suspended,
withdraws to a cracked crust.
Floods a high tidemark in grass.

How can I standing here
believe myself separate.
How can you standing there
believe yourself alone?

And the birds come in flocks and gather,
swoop and rise and stipple and roar,
all the flocks of the estuary in flight
on the dark of the world,
under a moon gazing round and speechless
on its crinkled echo.

Shepherd's Shore

You ask for the bus to stop. Then there's nothing
but a house, lonely. Behind it a green scar, the Wansdyke,
chalk blue butterflies gusting in clouds.
All the way to Tan Hill you walk their high white world.

Space is emptiness and company. Air is song and sting.
Earth a shaped body, its tramped distances the hike,
the thirst, the breathlessness. You've walked out
of everything the days assault you with, you've turned

off the only road for miles. Grass and stones, a ring
of megaliths for destination, a day to make you look,
the slow purple sky massing questions unheard
in the plain.   Past Shepherd's Shore the spurned

sun in hand, the moon on shoulder.
The way back longer than your time to wander.

There Are Places on the Downs that Turn You Back

Walking up from Avebury maybe, the day hot,
the pack heavy, white ruts of the track,
your mind numb and wide as the blue sky.
Nettled and itchy, stopping to drink, spilt water
a splashed glitter. Tiny blue butterflies
wispy on the scabious.
                           And then you look up
and see how the track rises and bends ahead,
a dark fringe of trees, rare here, conifers
planted by some farmer years ago,
and it's like a shadow falling on your heart,
a silent warning spoken. So you finish your drink
and think *I may never get here again* but still
hitch up the bag, turn round. Obey.

On First Hearing Beowulf

It was certainly raining,
the class room littered with pencils
no one could be bothered to pick up.
One pole-propped window dripping,
cabbagy with steam from the canteen.
One of those afternoons in the 1960s
dark with de Gualle and Aberfan.

The teacher was young, the book small.
Put your heads on the desks.
We sprawled, glad to be still, close our eyes
while the world skewed and the word-hoard spilled.
Outside, in a sloping yard,
mothers mourned the overwhelmed.

The beast roared out of the dark. I fought it,
with a wrench of sinews tore its arm from the socket,
hung it in the hall's rafters. Strode home,
careless through the drips
plopping in the cleaner's bucket. Didn't know,
running through a rare new kingdom,
I was a hero, one of the lucky ones.

The last monster comes later,
shrivels at each lamppost, vengeful and silent.
One day I'll turn and see the scaly reptilian darkness,
every street leading to its mound,
coiling and crushing, counting its stolen children.

Prehistoric Footprints

walk from there to here.
Stop midstride.
Fingered at each flood
by small
musings of water.

Two adults and a child,
the child running through sky
to a land no longer viable.
Forests under wave.
Drowned palaces.

Splatting the liquid mud,
splashing it on shins,
squelching between toes.

Very long ago, but I remember.
The centuries passing.
The turning to stone.

From the Mabinogi

1. Gronw Pebr Makes the Spear While the People are at Mass

The shaft is ash, planed smooth. Week by week
shavings, thin as paper, curl from it.
Between introit and Confiteor, I've brought it
to fit my hand. Hefted, tested it.
Summer, among birdsong,
I sweated in the clearing,
forging steel in a gloria of sparks.
In leaf-fall days I melted down my credo,
poured silver rivulets into a mould of clay.
Frost formed on me as I beat it out,
each blow against a man I've never seen,
for a woman dark as leaves, a petalled girl
rank and wanton as a hedgerow.
He can only die while not on land or sea.
Not clothed or naked, not inside or out.
Like all of us he thinks himself secure
but this blade I break at the sacring
all shining from its crock, will murder him.

Rehearse the blow, sweep the stroke,
feeling his scream, her tangled limbs round me.
The bells of the missa sending the people home,
the cars pulling away, her kiss like honey.

2. Branwen Chooses a Bird for her Message

Of all the birds she could have found
that it would be this one; needle-beaked
and cocky, one bright eye sidelong.
What would such speech be like?
All squeaks and squawks, cant and stab.
She must have found it harsh and quarrelsome,
the hysterics, the sardonic
scorn of its trills and tapers.
How could a princess
– even when a slave –
endure such outre repartee,
such arrogant greengloss strut?
She must have longed for a robin at least,
a gold-tongued blackbird, the nobility of hawks.
Yet she taught this one her tragedy
and he took the tale
in no flock, alone as never before,
over the green sea to the cloud-high ear
of her brooding brother.

The Building and the Boy

The building creaks a window down and listens.
Someone's climbing up the hill.
Someone's hacking through the thorns.

The building is alarmed.
All its corridors concerned.
This hasn't happened now for years.

The building leans towards the forest,
tilts, cautiously, its lichened tiles.
Gulls rise like hackles from its turrets.

A lover? A developer? A prince?
How can the building tell the difference?
Rats shiver in its rafters.

The building closes doors, prepares defences.
Gates slam with rusty slithers.
Spiders stitch webs over the locks.

He's climbed for years but now he's made it.
This is the edifice in every story.
He's left behind his family, his shadow.
He's young. Adventure makes him happy.
He calls out "I know you're there!
I know you're listening through these walls.
I'm Jack. I'm Tom. I'm all the sleeping princes.
I'm Childe Roland at the haunted tower.
I fully intend to make my mark on you."
Dark bricks loom behind the leaves.
He takes out water, gulps it down.
"Open up" he says. "I'm waiting."

The building thinks about its options.
Its long-laid plans are safe in storerooms.
Its cellars of contingency are strong.

It extrudes the thinnest bridge across the moat.
Grinds up the portcullis six rusty inches.
What can harm it? What can worry it?

He's so careful. Knows all the pitfalls,
has read the legends of the men who came before.
Corridors of darkness radiate.
Rooms on every side. He says
"I'm not here for treasure. I'm not here
to kiss a sleeping girl on cloth of gold.
I'm here for secrets and eternity."
No answer, but he knows the air is listening.
He leaves a trail of breadcrumbs,
unravels wool his mother made him bring,
marks corners with his name, doors with initials,
graffities the darkness with his energy,
blazes the stone with boldness and decision.

The building smiles. The building feels quite tickled.
Rather likes the artless images.
Closes the gate carefully. Withdraws the bridge.

He wanders a lifetime of tunnels, endless stairs.
Peers in at rooms of every size and décor.
"I know you're here" he says, but tired now.
No one told him it would be like this.
In books the heroes always have it easy,
princess or beast, you meet it fast,
and always some old woman, some black cat
gives you a spell, an answer, a way back.
He finds a bedroom and curls up to sleep,
one hand trailing from the sheets.

The building watches him snore and snuffle.
Arranges the spilt jigsaw of his dreams.
Fascinated, just a little fond,

causes a fire to crackle in the chimney.
Invisible hands spread food across a table.
Slippers warm by the coals.

He sits up in bed. He says "Oh no.
You'll never soften me into old age.
Send me monsters, send me minataurs,
torment me with howling and slammed doors,
ghostly girls that peep at me from mirrors."
But he's hungry. So he eats the food.
It tastes of brick-dust. It's a mistake.

That's it then. The building lets him wander,
teases with a few more secret tunnels,
sends the odd rat to make him jump.

It's over, far too easy.
Outside the wood's already grown again,
brambles tight, thorns thicker than before.

The building settles, muffles its shutters.
One day someone will come it might not handle,
a being who lingers at the edge of tales.

This isn't him. This one, like the others,
will take a lifetime and still leave
infinite black chambers unexplored.

Relieved, a little disappointed,
the building checks the padlock round its heart.
Blows out candles down its halls like stars.

Starlings

The poem bursts at sunset from the trees,
small black syllables wheeling in a flock,
frantic sounds. Abrupt, it veers
from shadow hawks, splits, panics,
crashes back, zigzags through rhymes
on crazy gasps and indrawn gulps of air,
brief migrant urges, patterns that won't form,
never stopping or getting anywhere
till about now.
              When the screeching cluster
breaks and comes down and dissolves,
to frail-boned consonants settling in rows;
preening, quarrelling, edging each other off.

Under their spiky fights and re-arrangements,
news and wars and love affairs transmit.

La Belle au Bois Dormant

1. Blood

Bead of blood rising like a dome.
Cabochon of blood from a thread of vein,
an artery, the deep heart.
Berry of blood dark as sloes,
put to the mouth and tasted.
Drawn off in needles and canulars
and the spindle that falls from your hand.
So tiny, but you sleep, you fall asleep
and while you sleep the world
grows wild. The hedges sprout,
the house is overwhelmed,
its towers tangled, its lawns jungles,
and you, a princess in a golden bed,
lie waiting for the one who might get through.
He might be good, he might be dangerous;
it will take centuries to know.
The berry blood will not coagulate,
never stop its drip,
till the alarm rings in the corridors
and the night prince
cuts through the wires and brambles,
hurries towards you in his whitest scrubs
and kisses it away.

2. Bramble King

He starts with a seed, the tiniest,
a malignant cell from who knows where,
but while you're sleeping he's at work,
growing, branching. His briars spring
and root where they touch,
in days he's a thicket round your heart.
Thorn-crowned, unaccountable,
all husk and pip and prickle,
his dance a swift stepping, there's no way
past him, even frost leaves him bare and lean,
the coldest moon sees him purposeful.
He's tapping your window.
Besieging your door. It will take angels,
it will take the spells of sorcerers to stop him,
because now the briar hedge out-tops the castle
and the wood is white with his roots.
While you worry he'll tap and tap
till the glass shatters and the casement cracks
and he's in. That king's kiss
sharp on your lips, draws blood,
his embrace kills you or cures you,
poisons or pleases you.
Maybe you'll never know which.

3. A Hundred Years

You have lain here so long
spiders have webbed your song.

You have lain here so still
your eyelids are petals.

Near your enchanted pillow
flies die in the window.

Only internet flickers
allow the world to enter.

Only remote cameras
show the impaled rescuers.

Every night the moon
undergoes its transformations,

every night you dream
of the holed tree, the stream.

Every day is a cut mark
in the skin's bark,

the poison corroding
all your imagining.

4. The Other Princes

The other princes are snagged in brambles,
their beautiful hair all thorn-combed,
their pale faces, their blue-cold eyes
closed against sharpness.
Swords rust, hunting horns are silent.

You've seen them, hung out to dry,
pinned like dragonflies, gold and bronze,
gagged with ivy, there where the moon
stabs the terrible hedge,
and the palace gleams like pearl.

Cross the fields, turn away, because how
can you ever untangle them?
How can you tell them the gates won't open,
can't ever be dragged wide
with the weight that's on them?

You can't whisper that in their ears.
They won't see or hear you
and you'd have to get right in among them,
squeeze right in and be caught up too,
all crooked, all sprawled.

O, the princes, impaled on silence.
Do they suffer? Do they sleep?
How will they feel when you scramble past them,
hallowed in magic, the thorns recoiling,
the bright key in your hand?

5. The Holed Tree

Before the treatment and the silence
she walked to the holed tree.
She put her eye to the place where the branch
loops a circle of air, and looked through.
There was the river and the wood,
and the sky dark with coming rain. It was good,
it was enough.

When it was over she came back,
as she'd sworn she would.
One of the set destinations in the long sleep,
one of the places in the world
she would walk to again.
The sky still dark, the river still running
but muddy now

the paths cow-trampled,
the snowdrops meekly contemplating
the earth they rose from.
Eye to the slit, she sees a world
different, maybe enchanted,
glass-edged and faceted, all bright,
the river not older,

not younger. As if it happened
to somebody else, as if the
spindle had not fallen out of her hand.
And yet there are scars, there are dreams,
the remembered rooms of the palace,
a century's silence. All the long nights
when they thought she slept

but she didn't.

The Clockwork Crow

He builds it from cogs and fear and worries
at night in his tower cell.
Its beak is wire, its claws
horn, its eye a jewel.

He spreads out its wings,
each feather a snagged space,
a tweezered interlace,
each a problem, a hollow barb.

His fingers, with tiny probes,
insert a small throbbing heart.
When the moon's full and the snow's falling
he'll wind it up, step back.

It will turn its head, speak one word.
Will rise, jerkily at first then
smooth, a shadow swooping under the ceiling,
beating against the window,

till he opens the glass
and lets it out, up into the stars and it flies
till it's a dark thing against the galaxies
and then is gone.

On Waiting

There are rooms designed for it
where you go between idea and action.
In this house it's a craft well practised
– the yawning cat, the unmended curtain.
In a small sloping row
of notebooks its drafts accumulate.
Degas' dancer on one brazen toe
might be posing for its mascot.
Grim determination, deferred pain.
In hospitals you see it everywhere,
an epidemic never to be cured.
Look, everyone in the bus queue in the rain
is dead from it, minds empty as umbrellas,
eyes fixed on the turn in the road.

St Blaize 2017

There are daffs out at Dyffryn Ardudwy,
and someone has cut his name
in a crooked tree at the station.

It's unreadable, long-lichened,
swollen to an ogham of slants and slashes,
closed like a bruised eye.

I feel at my neck the ghost of crossed candles,
a bardic blessing,
as a sheep blotched with one blue dot

looks up from the chequerboard
of pebbled walls.
I feel at my neck the cold lost wax,

the tap and rattle of candles, the red ribbon,
and I reach up and touch
but there's only a scarf against the cold.

And the thousand swallowed words,
the unsaid replies, the unspoken poems,
the names gone to silence in the throat,

that the bark of the years has grown over.
May you be protected the sheep say,
the birds sing, the speeding train roars.

Acknowledgements

Some of these poems have appeared in *The Rialto, Poetry Wales, The North, New Welsh Review.*

Well chosen words

Seren is an independent publisher with a wide-ranging list which includes poetry, fiction, biography, art, translation, criticism and history. Many of our books and authors have been on longlists and shortlists for – or won – major literary prizes, among them the Costa Award, the Jerwood Fiction Uncovered Prize, the Man Booker, the Desmond Elliott Prize, The Writers' Guild Award, Forward Prize and TS Eliot Prize.

At the heart of our list is a beautiful poem, a good story told well or an idea or history presented interestingly or provocatively. We're international in authorship and readership though our roots are here in Wales (Seren means Star in Welsh), where we prove that writers from a small country with an intricate culture have a worldwide relevance.

Our aim is to publish work of the highest literary and artistic merit that also succeeds commercially in a competitive, fast changing environment. You can help us achieve this goal by reading more of our books – available from all good bookshops and increasingly as e-books. You can also buy them at 20% discount from our website, and get monthly updates about forthcoming titles, readings, launches and other news about Seren and the authors we publish.

www.serenbooks.com